Femininity Lost and Regained

Femininity Lost and Regained

ROBERT A. JOHNSON

Harper Perennial
A Division of HarperCollins Publishers

First HarperPerennial edition published 1991.

The Library of Congress has catalogued the hardcover edition as follows:

Johnson, Robert A., 1921–
    Femininity lost and regained / Robert A. Johnson.—1st ed.
        p. cm.
    ISBN 0-06-016271-6
    1. Femininity (Psychology) 2. Femininity (Philosophy) 3. Femininity (Psychology) in literature. 4. Femininity (Philosophy) in literature. 5. Oedipus (Tale) 6. Nala (Hindu mythology) 7. Damayanti (Hindu mythology) I. Title.
BF175.5.F45J64 1990
155.3'33—dc20   89-45675

ISBN 0-06-092063-7 (pbk.)
91 92 93 94 95 FG 10 9 8 7 6 5 4 3 2 1

Contents

Femininity Lost and Regained

1

The Current Issue

The loss of feminine qualities and energy is an urgent psychological issue in modern society. It is a painful concern in the emotional lives of both men and women. This loss of something so essential for a woman forces her to question her femininity. It crystallizes the long historic debate about the position of women in society. The loss of feminine energy for a man is less obvious, but it curtails the emotional depths of his personality and is the source of much of his discontent, loneliness, sense of meaninglessness, and moodiness. It is a shock for a man to discover that his moods and much of his feeling nature are feminine! To be overtaken by a mood is to be overwhelmed by the inner feminine aspect of his character, and it is only by understanding and embracing this femininity that he can clearly understand his masculine nature. The loss or damage of inner feminine qualities affects our emotional well-being, directly modifying our happiness and contentment. If the feminine qualities are in good order, a person will feel safe and secure.

In understanding that femininity is not the prerogative of the female, our first task is to school ourselves to think of it as an entity that affects a woman's central feminine identity and affects a man's ability and capacity for feeling and valuing.

It would be easier to understand this vital dimension if our language were not so sexist and bankrupt. We lack terms for the feminine aspect of life that are multifaceted and rich. Languages often have several terms to describe the elements of a culture that are highly regarded. Conversely, if a language has few terms or a single one to describe an element of its cultural life, then low regard or value is sometimes indicated. For example, Sanskrit, the basis for most East Indian languages, has ninety-six terms for love. Ancient Persian has eighty, Greek has four, English only one. English does not have the breadth, scope, and differentiation for the feminine and for feeling experiences of Sanskrit and Persian. If it did, then we would have a specific word to use in our appreciation of father, mother, sunset, wife, house, mistress, or God. Having only one word to apply to these many levels of experience makes it difficult to understand the complexity of our inner lives and emotions. The Eskimo language has thirty words for snow. This reflects the need for clarity in a complex relationship to snow. When we are as interested in relationship and femininity as the Eskimo is in snow, we will evolve a differentiated and focused language for that dimension of our lives.

The mythologist Joseph Campbell tried to enlarge our discussion of femininity by invoking the following terms:

> the left, the side of the heart, the shield side, has been symbolic, traditionally and everywhere, of the feminine virtues and dangers: mothering and seduction, the tidal powers of the moon and substances of the body, the rhythms of the seasons: gestation, birth, nourishment, and fosterage; yet equally malice, and revenge, irrationality, dark and terrible wrath, black magic, poisons, sorcery, and delusion; but also fair enchantment, beauty, rapture, and bliss. And the right, thereby, is of the male: action, weapons, hero-deeds, protection, brute force, and both cruel and benevolent justice; the masculine virtues and dangers: egoism and aggression, lucid luminous reason, sunlike creative power but also cold unfeeling malice, abstract spirituality, blind courage, theoretical dedication, sober, unplayful moral force.*

Language forms our thought even when we think we are being open-minded. A friend of mine was preparing her final paper for the course work before ordination as an Episcopal priest. A daemon got into her and she decided to write from an entirely femi-

* Joseph Campbell, *Creative Mythology* (New York: Viking, 1968), pp. 288–89.

nine perspective—this in the face of the rigid patriarchal structure of the church. Her friends advised
strongly against this move, but she persevered. She
wrote:

> As a woman, writing a personal statement, I
> have chosen to use the term "woman" through-
> out this paper, but I wish it clearly understood
> that in this paper the term "woman" includes
> men as well, with no intention to exclude the
> male gender (except where the context clearly so
> indicates)—either from my understanding of
> theological anthropology and the nature of the
> church or, particularly, from the saving work of
> Jesus Christ. This is not done in complete inno-
> cence, of course. In part, I am attempting to re-
> verse, for myself and my readers, the experience
> of reading theology, which claims to include my
> gender but seldom does so.

Writing on the theological notion of the person, she
said:

> My sense of human nature is that woman is a
> finite creature (created being of God), who is ra-
> tional, spiritual, imaginative, and creative, or, as
> the Book of Common Prayer has it, "blessed . . .
> with memory, reason, and skill." She has free
> will (limited, but real) and potential to become a
> true child of God, transcending herself as she
> matures. In understanding her theologically, we
> must continually struggle to maintain a balance
> between her spiritual nature and her material
> nature, which has sometimes been "over-spirit-

ualized" by faith communities. Her goal is to love: herself, other women, and more importantly, God.

. . . I think we get the best picture of the purposes for which woman was created and the possibilities in her nature in the person of Jesus. We can only properly understand who woman is after seeing who Christ is, . . . because only in the light of the cross can we see the actual sinfulness of woman, as well as her potential destiny.

. . . Of all the created creatures we can see on earth, woman alone (as far as we know) has the power of reason and memory.

Further, there is in woman (preeminently seen in Jesus) what Karl Rahner calls "transcendental," the psalmist calls "a little lower than the angels," and Genesis calls "in the image of God."*

The word "men," meaning all mankind, in our scriptures and elsewhere has long subjected us to distortion. The semantic weight is toward maleness no matter what effort we make to include women in the term "men."

We must search out this elusive quality—femininity—and find something of its history, even given our paucity of language. Two attitudes—one Greek, the other Hindu—will help us understand the roots of femininity in modern civilization. The myth of Oedipus carries the Greek point of view, our imme-

---

* From responses to ordination examination questions by Jean Dalby Clift.

diate heritage; the myth of Nala and Damayanti, from the *Mahabharata*, conveys the East Indian attitude.

A NEW PERSPECTIVE

Our Western attitudes toward femininity are so deeply ingrained that it is impossible to gain perspective on them without going entirely outside our own culture. It was my journeys to India that wakened me to a vastly different outlook on everything feminine. The feeling tone, the valuation of femininity, occupy infinitely high places in the East Indian ethos. Just to walk on a street in traditional India is to walk in valid feeling. To experience as Indians do colors, tempi, sounds, sensuousness, relatedness, modesty, and timelessness is to be reminded of the Divine Feminine.

Our Western heroic achievements are the envy of the rest of the world, but they were won at the cost of our capacity for warmth, feeling, contentment, and serenity. We are so rich in things and so poor in feminine values! I saw peace and happiness in the most unexpected places in India! With so little to be happy about, how is it that these people are so contented? At the cost of modern technical accomplishments, they have maintained their feminine values.

The myth of Nala and Damayanti comes strange to Western ears, but that strangeness is the exact quality we need to round out our disastrously one-sided Western way of life. In this East Indian myth, women of strong feminine identity avert disaster. Inescapably, it is feminine strength that is the hero. The Hindu stories simply would not work without the power of their women—the power of the *feminine*, for it is not confined to women alone.

Instinctively we Westerners know that there is an essential ingredient in the East that we need in order to cure our emotionally impoverished Western culture. Eastern philosophy and religion have become familiar to us since the 1960s, whether from political radicals or from eminent scientists. J. Robert Oppenheimer's book detailing the development of the first atomic bomb was titled *Brighter Than a Thousand Suns*, a quote from the Upanishads. Works of fiction such as Hermann Hesse's *Siddhartha* and Somerset Maugham's *The Razor's Edge* have explored curative aspects of Eastern thought. It is in this manner that we can learn from the tale of Nala and Damayanti.

1

The Feminine in Western Culture

2

The Greek Heritage

✺✺✺

So much of our cultural and philosophical heritage has its origin in ancient Greece; our science, our political ideas, much of our language, and many of our customs come from that great flowering which was the glory of Athens about 500 B.C. Many of our cherished cultural possessions bear Greek names—*democracy*, *aristocracy*, *psychology*, *politics*, *ecstasy*, *mystery*—and numerous medical and scientific terms are Greek in origin. It has been said that all philosophy since Greek times has been but a footnote to Plato.

But there is a dark note in our Greek heritage that is not often recognized or understood. The glory that was Greece and that still illumines our civilization was bought at a very high price—a price paid daily by every one of us and rarely attributed to its source.

We have begun questioning the patriarchal form of

Western culture, and it is thus that we first challenge our Greek heritage. True, the Greeks honored the feminine in seven goddesses, corresponding to the seven gods; but in everyday life, Greece had a patriarchal structure, and femininity suffered a blow so wounding that it has not yet recovered. Much of our emotional lives is that unhealed wound still festering.

It is inevitable that a "high" civilization like Greece should exact an equally high—or deep—price. The feminine, ignominious in its suffering, paid the price, while the masculine gloried in its attainments. Perhaps a wiser race could have paid this blood price in a better way, but that would be to ask what humanity as a whole has not been able to accomplish to this day. It remains for us now—humanity at the present point in its evolution—to pay this price and evolve in a healthier way than any of our ancestors devised.

Greece was not alone in its degrading of the feminine; the Hebrew world also denied the feminine, and lesser cultures hardly acknowledged it. The Hebrews, like the Greeks, held the feminine in high esteem theoretically. The Shekinah—the presence of God in the world—was no less than the feminine half of God. But in practice, Judaism was a patriarchal institution that made the feminine pay the price for towering masculine accomplishment.

We can be grateful for that accomplishment; our world would be the poorer by half if it were pulled down. Science would be overturned; medicine and all the mechanical marvels of our time would vanish. We would "manure the field thou plowest," according to Mephistopheles in Goethe's *Faust*. Though we have begun to restore woman's place in our modern world, we have not done nearly enough in restoring the feminine—the values of feeling, peace, contentment, and perspective. There are voices in our society now that advocate reducing our suffering and alienation through a return to nature. Gandhi, the Amish, Rousseau, Thoreau, as well as certain of the 1960s hippies, espoused simpler ways of life to bring us closer to our succoring mother, the earth.

Perhaps thus would our pain be relieved, but at the cost of the very best of the modern world. A better way would be to pay the cost of what we have won in a more conscious way and by that cost-consciousness win the best of both masculine and feminine genius. If there is a better age—a millennium—to come, it would emerge out of this conscious appreciation of both values rather than from a violent swinging of the pendulum from one imbalance to another.

3

The Voice of Sophocles

Our search for the consciousness we seek begins with an inquiry into the history of the present masculine-feminine imbalance. The Greek culture left a chronicle of its attitudes in the story of Oedipus, which exemplifies Greece at its best—and at its worst. If we can understand this story of tragic nobility, we will be better equipped to see our own dilemma. The Indian myth of Nala and Damayanti contains many of the same elements, but they are worked out quite differently: the feminine is also treated badly, but the outcome contrasts with that of the Western story. Juxtaposing the two stories is intended not to prove one right and the other wrong but to expand our consciousness.

It is only by becoming more psychologically conscious that we can become more responsible. This is inner work that demands a high price in suffering, but we must pay that price in order to guarantee the evolution of our individual maturity and the intellectual and emotional flowering of our culture. The story of Oedipus is dramatized in the Theban Plays, by Sophocles.* Born in 496 B.C., the Greek dramatist lived through some of the most tumultuous times recorded in history: the rise of Greece to its full power, the Peloponnesian wars, which bled this high civilization nearly dry, and the beginning of the decline that soon swept Greece into civil war and collapse. The plays concern the royal House of Thebes and the imposition of masculine law at the expense of feminine love and relatedness. This catastrophe reverberates through history to our own day.

According to legend, Cadmus, the father of the Theban empire, founds a city, but a dragon devours the first citizens. Cadmus kills the dragon with one stroke of his sword and sows its teeth within the city walls. They immediately spring up as giants so fierce that they begin killing each other. Only five are left, and these are the founders of Thebes. A purely masculine creation myth!

Generations later, Oedipus is born to be king of Thebes. An oracle says he will kill his father and marry his mother. In response, Oedipus' parents are obligated to kill him, but instead, inclined to kindness and humanity, they put an iron pin through his feet and order a servant to abandon him at the traditional

---

* Sophocles, *The Theban Plays* (New York: Viking Penguin, 1947).

place of exposure.* The servant, a shepherd, is unable to leave the child to die and gives him to a fellow shepherd, who takes the outcast to a neighboring kingdom. The king there has no son and takes the child as his own, naming him Oedipus—"swollen foot."

Early in his adulthood, Oedipus learns of the oracle's prediction and he flees his homeland to avert the ordained fate. After wandering for some time, he arrives in Thebes, his birthplace. There, he murders a man he encounters on the road. This man is his father, and the first part of the prophecy is fulfilled. Oedipus settles in the city but finds it in turmoil. Their king has been slain (by Oedipus), and the Sphinx, a hybrid monster, has taken possession of the land. The Sphinx asks a riddle, which no one can answer, and many are killed as the penalty of failure. Oedipus answers the riddle, saves the land from the Sphinx, and is given the widowed queen as his bride in recompense. The second part of the prophecy is thus fulfilled. The royal pair have two sons and two daughters, and Thebes is at peace for a time.

THE FATE OF FEMININITY

The Swiss psychologist C. G. Jung observed that the unconscious dimension of our psyche will show to us

---

* It was the ancient Greek custom to leave unwanted or deformed children at a particular place, to die of exposure if no one came searching for a child to adopt. Thus the life of the child was left to the disposition of the Fates.

the same face that we first show to it. If we have been hostile to it, it will be hostile to us. So much of our psychological life is a dialogue between our conscious world—all the things we know about ourselves—and the unconscious—the murky world of our interior life, which is such a mystery to us.

The first human act of the story brings an immediate reply from the chthonic, feminine forces of the inner world. When Cadmus, the legendary king, founds a city, mankind imposes masculine order, which we associate with culture and civil law.* But masculinity imposes form and order upon the land without making provision for the feminine elements of matter and earthiness, and the earth strikes back in the form of a dragon that nearly destroys the city. Cadmus kills the dragon, sows its teeth in the land of the new city, and raises the first generation of citizens—giants who immediately begin to kill each other. The five survivors are the founders of the city, which now is populated by the offspring of order and form (the legacy of Cadmus) and by the earth element, in the form of dragon teeth. Balance is restored, and the city can proceed in its development.

This is a wonderful prescription to remedy the life tension that nearly every modern person experiences. We work very hard (and Westerners work harder

---

* The prescription for founding a Greek city is interesting: Dig a well, which is the center of the city; then cut a continuous strip from an oxhide and set this in a circle around the well. The circumference of the circle will constitute the outer limits of the city.

than any people known in history) for our masculine, patriarchal achievement. This is "founding the city" and is a specifically masculine accomplishment. It is the pride and joy of the Western world! But the myth tells us that it is only half of reality and the feminine—that boundless, formless aspect of reality—will destroy the new masculine creation if it is not honored and drawn into the creation. The excluded feminine, now a dragon because it has been offended, threatens to bring the whole project down in ruins. A friend of mine, overweeningly proud of his recent accomplishment in a difficult business situation, behaved like a bantam rooster and made much of his achievement. But his wife, forced into a dragon role, instinctively punctured his masculine arrogance.

Cadmus exercises great wisdom in founding his city with both form (the well and the oxhide strip) and chaos (the dragon teeth). This ancient wisdom is an apt prescription for our everyday masculine accomplishments. Add dragon teeth to your triumphs; then true creation can take place. Men or women who add the inner feminine energy to patriarchal accomplishment court genius. The merger can take the form of a quiet half hour, a gift, a ceremony, or a libation to the feminine half of the patriarchal creation.

4

The Oedipal Story

The drumbeat of fate resounds like a leitmotif throughout the tale of Oedipus. It is decreed by the oracle that the king and queen of Thebes shall bear a son who will kill his father and marry his mother. To our view, there could hardly be a worse disaster. But remember that this is a king and queen, and—even more difficult—bear in mind that this is the history of inner consciousness, containing the laws and safeguards necessary for the advent of this consciousness. One hero, Oedipus, does it correctly and ushers in the golden age of Athens. Another, Creon, does it wrongly and ends in total isolation; the women of the story pay for his error.

The king and queen, hearing the prophecy, understandably attempt to circumvent the doom. No one wants consciousness; it comes to us only by fate and then only if we participate in the process and pay the whole price. They injure their child by putting an iron pin through his ankles and instruct a servant to take him to the place of exposure where unwanted or crippled children are left to die. This is a fine touch, for it leaves a cranny through which fate may speak. They don't kill the child but leave it to die.

The servant cannot bear to let the child die of exposure. He gives the boy to a shepherd, who takes him to another land. Here is a kind and human act, one of the slender feminine threads that constitute the strands of fate. The king and queen of the new land have no son and take Oedipus as their own. He grows up happily. Over the years, disturbing stories about his birth arise. He finally leaves his foster parents (he thinks they are his true parents) to escape the dreadful sentence, but this act only becomes the next strand of fate.

An Arab story tells clearly how the art of evasion is often the next thread of fate falling into its appointed place. A wealthy man in Mecca consulted a fortune-teller, who screamed and fainted when she looked into her crystal ball. This was not reassuring, and the man was frantic with worry when he finally got the fortuneteller revived. She informed him, when she could speak again, that death would meet him at the sunrise gate of Mecca at dawn. The man, exercising all the power his wealth provided, hired a caravan that night and was at the eastern gate of Agra by morning. There stood Death, waiting for him. "But I thought you were waiting for me at the gate of Mecca!" stuttered the man. "No," said Death. "It has been written for a thousand years that we should meet at the gate of Agra on this morning." By all the power of his wealth and the mistaken folly of the fortuneteller, he had made his way to the place of his death—all the time thinking he was evading death.

Thus, too, the king and queen of Thebes, trying to get rid of their fated child; and Oedipus, seeking to escape his fate by fleeing from his adopted parents. Both of these evasions only place Oedipus exactly where he must be to accomplish the terrible and wonderful fate that was announced before his birth.

Now the weight of consciousness falls upon Oedipus in the progression of his life. He has control of the details, but fate holds the main threads and rules with an iron hand, just as iron first bound his feet. He must pay his debt; the degree to which he does this allows consciousness to emerge, and he follows the path of nobility to create a golden age of Athens. But as he evades, he compounds the darkness and raises the price.

THE BLIND PROPHET

The story weaves its pattern as Oedipus flees his adopted land and finds his way, unknowingly, to Thebes, his native land. As the gentle Oedipus enters his true homeland, he is challenged by a band of travelers and, in defending himself, kills the leader of the band. Unknown to Oedipus, this man is his father, Laius, king of Thebes.

Arriving in the city, Oedipus finds Thebes under the spell of a deadly monster, the Sphinx, who has been destroying all who could not answer a cunning riddle she set before them. The Sphinx has gained power over the land because the great King Laius has been killed. The Sphinx is the next stage of the feminine monster who nearly destroyed Thebes at its founding. The denied feminine has progressed from a devouring dragon to a test of consciousness. The newcomer, Oedipus, is entreated to find the answer to the Sphinx's riddle. Succeeding, he delivers the land from its oppression. The people appoint him to be king and give him the wife of the former king as his own. Thus is fulfilled the terrible prophecy that Oedipus would kill his father and marry his mother.

Peace and harmony reign under Oedipus' wise rule for the space of fifteen years. But beneath the deceptive surface lies the hideous shame of Oedipus' secret, of which he knows only part. Another tyranny overwhelms the country, in the form of drought and pestilence, for the gods cannot leave so much darkness unattended for long.

Oedipus calls upon the gods to show the cause for the affliction of Thebes, and the oracle tells of the foul murder of their king, Laius. It is for this that the country now lies in oppression. Oedipus vows that the one who killed Laius shall be brought to justice and the country cleansed of so dark a deed.

A blind prophet is brought to reveal his inner vision and at first refuses to comment on what he knows. "I refuse to utter the heavy secrets of my soul—and yours."

And: "Do not blame me; put your own house in order."

The blind prophet finally tells the story of Oedipus, the son of Laius and Jocasta, banished to a foreign land, returning to kill his father and marry his mother, now standing accusing and accused as king of Thebes.

> The killer of Laius—that man is here:
> Passing for an alien, a sojourner here among us;
> But, as presently shall appear, a Theban born,
> To his cost. He that came seeing, blind shall
>   he go;
> Rich now, then a beggar; stick in hand, groping
>   his way
> To a land of Exile; brother, as it shall be shown,
> And father, at once, to the children he cherishes;
>   son,
> And husband, to the woman who bore him;
>   father-killer,
> And father-supplanter.
> Go in and think on this.
> When you can prove me wrong, then call me
>   blind.

Jocasta is summoned and after questioning becomes aware that Oedipus, now her husband, is her son. Oedipus acknowledges his terrible, though unconscious, acts and demands to be exiled from Thebes.

Jocasta, having learned of her unwitting part in the tragedy, hangs herself, thus paying out her guilt. Oedipus, in the first flush of his own guilt, snatches the golden brooches from her dress and thrusts them into his own eyes to extinguish the sight of the wife-mother, which so revolts him. By this shedding of his blood he makes the first atonement for his incestuous guilt.

Oedipus, by his own decree, is banished as king of Thebes, and Creon, the brother of Jocasta, takes the throne.

5

The Inner Meaning of Incest

To understand the tremendous impact of this story, we must firmly establish that it is an inner story and has little to do with literal fact. The fullest meaning will be found by interpreting the events as happening deep within a culture and, if we have the courage, within our own psychic history. This and stories like it all over the world from many times in history are psychic maps to guide the human soul in its perilous adventure toward consciousness.

The tale is not about prohibitions against literal incest but is like a dream, which offers guidance and safeguards for the establishment of consciousness. Stated as simply as possible, incest is the psychological act of making consciousness. It is when we turn the flow of our instinctual energy back upon itself that we make consciousness, the ability of the self to see itself. All our consciousness is won by this means. Every time we discipline ourselves, sit down and will ourselves to grow, we are committing incest, in an inner sense—mating with ourselves. We take a part of ourselves, embrace it, and engage in the divine act of becoming conscious. This is portrayed in pharaonic Egypt in a most striking manner. Ordinary people in that ancient culture were absolutely forbidden to marry within their family, under threat of immediate death. But the pharaoh was required to marry his sister! He could have no other wife. This was to force consciousness upon the aristocracy and to protect the people from such a powerful experience, which they might not be able to endure. Most cultures prescribe consciousness for their aristocracy but make careful prohibitions against this faculty for their common people. It is, then, the aristocratic part of ourselves that is destined to move toward consciousness, while the ordinary part of us obeys the basic laws and stays within conventional patterns.

All introversion (that psychological orientation which cares more about the inner life than about the external world) is incestuous, which is the reason that it is so suspect in the modern world. In fact, "morbid" and "introspection" are often paired in our modern thinking. It was Jung who coined the terms "introvert" and "extrovert." They describe different types of personalities or orientations toward life. In a primarily extroverted society like America's, most introverts are seen as out of synch.

When you go off to meditate or simply to refresh yourself after work or community, you are mating with yourself. One stream of energy is being introduced to another stream of energy, and their fusion produces an offspring, which, like a physical child, has the characteristics of the two parent energies but is independent of and often superordinate to both.

To engage in any discipline, to depart from the natural flow of energies, is to mate with yourself. There is an alchemical proverb: "I looked at myself, I mated with myself, I gestated myself, I gave birth to myself, I am myself." This is the act of self-generation.

It is an extremely dangerous activity and must be undertaken with great care, or a particularly vicious kind of destruction takes place instead of the birth of consciousness. The old maxim "The devil finds use for idle hands" is true for anyone unable to obey the laws of consciousness. Consciousness is an aristo-cratic prerogative and must be engaged in under the most careful circumstances. To disobey the natural laws of exogamous energy is permitted only to those who are destined to make high consciousness. The high price of commitment and psychological suffer-ing concerns most of the literature surrounding the art of personal growth and maturation.

And if this age into which we are entering can be characterized by a new consciousness then it is not surprising that incest would be very important to that new consciousness as a metaphor for inner conscious growth. The use of incest as a symbolic act, as a met-aphor for inner sight, is so new to us and our day that we are blind to this dimension of creativity. So we experience grave misunderstandings of this psychic reality. The sudden explosion of incest in its raw literal form screams at us from the media and litters our counseling offices. Never before has there been such an awareness of its pervasiveness and its growing incidence. Incest, molestation, and sexual exploitation are graphic examples of the golden touch of an emerging inner consciousness being acted out unconsciously in pathological and destructive ways. It is absolutely essential that our capacity for "incest" be used on its creative level—that of creating consciousness and culture. It should be safeguarded from its literal expression, which is so destructive to the human psyche.

It is the cost of disobeying the laws of the natural flow of energy that is the heart and soul of the Oedipus story. The inner journey toward growing consciousness is the hero's quest. Those who make the journey contribute to the growth of a culture. Any who misunderstand or cheat, refusing or failing to pay the cost of inner growth, pay instead in the coin of loneliness, anxiety, and alienation. It is chiefly the feminine that pays this inauthentic price.

THE BANISHMENT

Oedipus is finally banished from his kingdom. His two sons do nothing to aid their father and all but disown him. They are consumed by the drive to acquire power. One son, Eteocles, rebels against Creon, Oedipus' successor, and tries to wrest the power of the kingdom from him. The other, Polynices, goes to a neighboring kingdom, marries the daughter of the king, and makes war on his homeland to gain the throne of Thebes.

Oedipus' two daughters remain loyal. While Ismene stays in Thebes, seeking order, Antigone accompanies her father to the small kingdom of Colonus, near Athens, where they hope to live in peace and find redemption from their suffering. Oedipus remarks that "Three masters—pain, time, and the royalty in the blood—have taught me patience."

Oedipus learns that his two sons have engaged in a power struggle, first with Creon and then with each other. Locked in a battle to the death for their homeland, the sons say openly that they would rather have power over Thebes than have their father return. Oedipus responds:

> Only these two, my daughters,
> Have done all that women could, to give
>   me what I need,
> Food, and safe conduct, and their loving care.
> Their brothers sold their father for a throne,
> Preferred the scepter and the kingly power.

The oracle at Delphi has ordained that Oedipus is to be buried just outside Athens, so that his power will bring about a great cultural flowering for the city.

Ismene, the younger daughter, having come to Colonus, imparts to her father the oracle's decree. Oedipus asks: "Am I made man in the hour when I cease to be?" Ismene replies: "If the gods, who cast you down, now raise you up." Oedipus pledges his body to Athens.

Creon, who formerly enforced Oedipus' exile, now comes and demands his body to bring peace to Thebes. When Oedipus refuses, Creon announces that he has one of Oedipus' daughters as hostage and will kidnap the other to effect his plan. In a dreadful scene, the blind Oedipus listens helplessly while Creon abducts Antigone by brute force.

> CREON (*to his men*): Arrest her [Antigone]. Force her if she will not come.
> ANTIGONE: O help! O help me, gods and men.
> CHORUS: Stop, sir.
> CREON: The man is yours; but she is mine.
> CHORUS: You have no right.
> CREON: I have.
> CHORUS: What right?
> CREON: She's mine. (*He lays hands on her. The guards carry her away.*)

Creon then attempts to abduct Oedipus. Theseus, king of Athens, comes on the scene, saves Oedipus, recovers the two daughters from Creon's soldiers, and brings them back to Oedipus.

Oedipus speaks to his daughters just before his death:

This is the end of all that was I, and the end
of your long task of caring for me. I know how
hard it was.
Yet it was made lighter by one word—love.
I loved you as no one else had ever done.

They weep, clinging to each other. Then there is
silence, until suddenly a voice is heard, a terrifying
voice at which all tremble, their hair on end. "Oedipus! Oedipus!" it cries, again and again. "It is time:
you stay too long." Oedipus recognizes the summons
as from a god. He calls for King Theseus, and when
he comes near, addresses him: "Dear friend, give
your hand and promise to these children. Children,
your hand in his. Promise never of your own will to
forsake them, but do such things as you think fitting
for their good, with all goodwill." And the noble Theseus makes no lament but takes his oath to do as his
friend desires. Oedipus can die in peace.

> CHORUS (*commenting on Oedipus' death*): By some
>   act of god was it? And with no pain?
> MESSENGER: It was wonderful.

After Oedipus' burial, Antigone wants to see her
father's grave, but Theseus tells her that no one may
see the place of burial of the one who has given his
life for the cultural enrichment of a land. For such a
death is entirely impersonal and carries no value on
the ordinary human level.

✎

The very heart of the story is laid bare in the above passages. A man has been called by fate to create consciousness by the inward act of self-generation, and as a noble being he pays the price. He first accepts responsibility for what he has done, then suffers the consequences. His blindness—the voluntary relinquishing of sight to gain insight—is the principal price; but the payment also includes banishment from his former kingdom, loss of most of the masculine elements, which had sustained him previously, and the breakdown of the traditional hereditary ties.

Anyone who undergoes a development of consciousness is immediately assailed by a sense of abandonment and excommunication from most of the values that formerly sustained one. The old kingdom dissolves beneath such a one, who is left to feel exiled and without any container for life. The masculine elements are particularly hostile to any change in consciousness. It has been said that Jesus had no trouble with the women near him but came to grief with the prevailing masculine law and order of his time.

The first glimmer of hope that Oedipus' suffering is of value comes from the oracle of Delphi. Oedipus is to be buried at the outskirts of Athens, for the great enrichment of that city. An ironic touch! He is not to be buried in state within the city, but only on the edge, where his spirit will guide Athens to its golden age without the acclaim of an official hero.

Here is the heart of our story. If someone destined to achieve a degree of consciousness will pay the price for it, there will ensue a great cultural flowering. It is not that the ego is raised to great creative heights but that the achievement of consciousness brings an efflorescence nearby. Oedipus does little but suffer; it is Athens that flourishes.

Oedipus had vowed to search out the one whose guilt brought calamity on the kingdom of Thebes. He remained loyal to his word even when he discovered it was he himself who was the guilty one. One experiences much collective guilt when embarking on the individual path of consciousness. It is necessary to distinguish collective guilt from individual guilt. We must take responsibility for our own guilt, but we must refuse the guilt that originates outside. We are all burdened with a heavy weight of the sins of our forebears or of the culture in which we live, but we must not take personal responsibility for this. It is basic and sound theology that we are guilty only of those things that we have originated. The darkness of this story did not originate with Oedipus, so he did not need to assume personal responsibility for it.

But Oedipus does blind himself upon hearing of his guilt. This indicates that the sight once focused outward to the everyday world has been translated to insight, the focus on cultural creativity, which is the whole meaning of the story. The glory that was Athens derived from the nobility of a man chosen by fate for a cultural process, a man willing to pay the price and make good the prophecy. Interpreted internally, as is necessary in uncovering the true dimensions of a story or myth, this means that the center of one's being is enriched by the work done by the conscious personality. Little value falls to the ego, which paid the price for the transformation. Athens will flower in creativity because a man paid the price of consciousness.

THE EVASION OF RESPONSIBILITY

We have witnessed the nobility of a man who is destined by fate to help people achieve understanding and evolve to a higher level of consciousness. He suffers terribly, but he wins a creativity worth more than gold. That creativity is more than his own personal possession, for the myth tells us that all Athens was made great by his creation of consciousness. Spiritual and emotional responsibility is what causes this creative growth in consciousness. Oedipus paid for his new consciousness and created in himself a golden age—reflected in the glory of Athens.

As Westerners, we have yet to learn that every action sets off a counteraction at the opposite end of the scale. It is as if we live on a seesaw, with the fulcrum in the exact center. Any action on the right-hand side of the seesaw will instantly set up a counterbalancing action on the left-hand side. A high cultural achievement will engender a corresponding darkness. A creation sets in motion a corresponding destruction. The cultural or creative act can be maintained if its corresponding opposite is honored and given equal consciousness. We are so abysmally unaware of this law that we have no adequate language for it. How can you say that you must destroy as much as you create without sounding as if you were denying the whole cultural process? To create without paying tribute to destruction is as impossible as attempting to breathe in without breathing out. Significantly, it is wise that Good Friday precedes Easter Sunday.

The legacy of creation that Oedipus leaves us is the glory of Athens—all its nobility of thought and philosophy, its political insights and artistry. No greater flowering of culture has happened on the face of the earth at any time in history. But no corresponding tribute to the dark side of reality accompanied it. It is the failure to comprehend this dark side that has led to so much darkness since. The fact that we have no language or concept for darkness that gives it equal dignity with lightness is the root of our problem. I sit at a keyboard, incapable of giving beauty and nobility to the other half of creation.

THE TRANSFER

We come now to a dark passage in our story. Oedipus reveals his nobility by paying the price of his evolution, but three other men do not pay the price and transfer it to women. This evasion reverberates through history and is present in our own time. Modern women feel unjustly burdened with something not of their own origin. They feel this evasion, which is largely our dark heritage from Greece. An enterprising group of people raised a high civilization, the golden age of Athens, but failed to pay the price for it, and left us both genius and damaged femininity as a legacy.

The story of the three other men is instructive: Creon, who showed Oedipus very little compassion during his trial, immediately took advantage of his suffering and appointed himself king of Thebes as soon as he had exiled the former ruler. Where love must compete with power, love perishes. Creon, mad for power, lacked compassion. Although he repented at the end and tried to help Antigone, it was too late.

The two sons of Oedipus hardly have their father in his grave before they quarrel over the right of accession to the throne. They fight and kill each other in a single day.

Each of the three men wounds the women close to him. Creon takes a path of power that will bring about the death of his wife and his prospective daughter-in-law. Oedipus' two sons relinquish any love for their father and sisters and kill each other in a power struggle. It is here that we see a noble path degenerate into a denial of feminine values. This denial haunts us to this day. The pursuit of power is the most serious danger that faces feminine values. Creon, Polynices, and Eteocles supplant Oedipus and turn our story from a noble tale of the evolution of consciousness into a lust for power that destroys relationship, love, and devotion.

The two daughters make wiser choices about life. Antigone maintains unquestioned loyalty to her father, and Ismene stays as close to him as her sense of practicality allows. We can now follow these two women in their modeling of feminine values.

6

The Fate of Antigone

As is so often the case in human history, war erupts over the drive for power. Eteocles, who wants the kingship of Thebes, defends the city against Polynices, who attempts to take possession of it. The brothers kill each other, and Creon is left undisputed ruler of Thebes. He issues an edict that Eteocles is to be honored and given a proper burial, but anyone who attempts to take Polynices' body from the battlefield will be killed. Polynices is to be left in dishonor on the battlefield and eaten by the vultures. The city obeys this edict.

Antigone asks the help of Ismene to bury Polynices, her brother, but she refuses; it would not be practical. Antigone says: "Live, if you will; live, and defy the holiest laws of heaven." Ismene replies: "May the dead forgive me, I can do no other but as I am commanded; to do more is madness."

Creon finds that Polynices' body has been given

burial. He orders the man bringing this news to find the perpetrator, under penalty of torture. Antigone is caught covering over her brother's body and is brought to Creon.

CREON: Now tell me, in as few words as you can,
    Did you know the order forbidding such an
      act?
ANTIGONE: I knew it, naturally. It was plain
    enough.
CREON: And yet you dared to contravene it?
ANTIGONE: Yes.
    That order did not come from God. Justice,
    That dwells with the gods below,
      knows no such law.
    I did not think your edicts strong enough
    To overrule the unwritten unalterable laws
    Of God and heaven, you being only a man.
    They are not of yesterday or today,
      but everlasting,
    Though where they came from,
      none of us can tell.
    Guilty of their transgression before God
    I cannot be, for any man on earth.
    I knew that I should have to die, of course,
    With or without your order. If it be soon,
    So much the better. Living in daily torment
    As I do, who would not be glad to die?
    This punishment will not be any pain.
    Only if I had let my mother's son
    Lie there unburied,
      then I could not have borne it.
    This I can bear. Does that seem foolish to you?

Or is it you that are foolish to judge me so?
My way is to share my love, not share my hate.
CREON: Go then,
    and share your love among the dead.
We'll have no woman's law here, while I live.

Here is the direct collision of the dominant masculine point of view—power—and the feminine capacity for love and devotion. If love had prevailed, Western history would have had a very different course. Perhaps the outcome was inevitable at that stage of human development, the masculine lust for power proving greater than the feminine vision of relatedness. Creon orders death for both sisters.

Earlier in the story, Antigone had been betrothed to Haemon, Creon's son. Since Antigone's fate concerns Haemon, he is summoned.

CREON: Son, you have heard, I think, of our
    final judgment on your late betrothed.
    No angry words, I hope?
    Still friends, in spite of everything, my son?
HAEMON: I am your son, sir; by your wise decisions
    My life is ruled, and them I shall always obey.
    I cannot value any marriage tie
    Above your own good guidance.
CREON: Rightly said.
    Your father's will should have your heart's first
    place.
    Only for this do fathers pray for sons
    Obedient, loyal, ready to strike down

Their father's foes, and love their father's
    friends. . . .
He whom the State appoints must be obeyed
To the smallest matter, be it right—or wrong.

Here a weak man is coerced by masculine authority, and though he knows better (and will show his
true feelings when it is too late), he makes no protest
when faced with his father's abject cruelty. The example is set for succeeding generations, down to our
own. This sentiment—or lack of it—has been used
often in recent history. The predominant reply of
those accused at the Nuremberg war trials was: "I
was only following orders." Human feeling is persis-
tently eclipsed by authority.

Creon banishes Antigone to a rock-vaulted tomb,
where she is left with a month's supply of food, even-
tually to starve to death—this so that the blood guilt
will not be on the king of Thebes.

Creon consults an oracle, which warns him of the
consequences of his cruelty. He buries the body of
Polynices with all due rites. Then he goes to the cave
where he has imprisoned Antigone, but arrives to find
she has hanged herself. Haemon, enraged at the loss
of his beloved, tries to kill his father. Failing at this, he
turns his sword on himself. Creon's wife, Eurydice,
kills herself upon learning of her son's death.

The play ends as Creon, responsible for his son's
death and thereby for his wife's, stands in the center
of the stage, completely alone, all the feminine ele-

ments destroyed, his entire family killed, and Thebes
brought to ruin. He speaks:

> I am nothing. I have no life.
> Lead me away,
> That have killed unwittingly
> My son, my wife.
> I know not where I should turn,
> Where to look for help.
> My hands have done amiss, my head is bowed,
> With fate too heavy for me.

7

The Oedipal Legacy

The myth of Oedipus, central to Greek mythology, tells us in brief and simple form the wonderful and terrible legacy we have inherited from our spiritual parent, Greece. It is the story of a fateful moment in the life of humanity—the first appearance of the modern mind-set. Fate decreed that a man should learn the secrets of incest and, by paying the emotional and physical price for that knowledge, lay the foundations for the glory of Athens. The noble Oedipus paid that price and gave his gift to Athens, to the Athens that is not so much a city as a way of life, an attitude, a particular kind of consciousness. At our best, we are citizens of Athens to this day.

But another man, Creon, had the same opportunity and failed. These two instruct us on how to cope with our dual legacy of light and dark, noble and tragic, loving and cruel.

The great lesson we must learn has to do with human responsibility. Oedipus paid the price for his new consciousness; Creon made the women and the feminine elements around him pay his price. Nothing seems more dishonorable or inhumane to us than to make someone else, who is innocent, pay for our mistakes and faults. Be it a domestic quarrel or an international incident, the subject is often that of price. It is a flaw in a man—fatal unless he wakens to it—that he carefully arranges life so that the feminine will pay the price for his masculine creation. He may have his high moment of sexuality and walk away, leaving the woman to cope with the practicality; or he may use the materials of the world for his own ends and leave a ravaged planet, out of balance and malfunctioning. Worst of all, because it is so subtle, he may take the high stuff of consciousness and leave the feminine within himself to pay the price: inner darkness and meaninglessness. It is this latter that we must investigate.

Oedipus acknowledges his inner vision (described as incest in our story) and bears the responsibility for it. He clearly announces that he will bring the one responsible for the decline of Thebes to justice; and when he discovers that one to be himself, he asks to be exiled and suffers the full impact of the loss of his homeland—that is, of the consciousness he knew before his insight. The acquisition of a new vision requires the sacrifice of the old. Painfully, Oedipus destroys his old sight and directs his energy in a new direction, via insight. To take this part of the story literally is to lose its deepest meaning. The blinding of Oedipus is meant to illustrate an inner truth, much as the symbols in a dream do. He is directed away from the old focus and the old attitudes. Faust goes through the same redirection near the end of his story, when Dame Care blinds him.* One of the noblest acts a man can perform is to keep his consciousness and his attitudes at a level and direction appropriate to his current stage of development. To pretend he is more advanced than he really is causes psychological splits; yet to refuse to grow always forces someone else to pay for one's psychological debts. As I have said, this is one of the darkest of human capacities.

Creon fails exactly where Oedipus proves his nobility. Creon wants power in the old way and directs his energy into old patterns. To this end, he assumes control of the kingdom, battles with Oedipus' two sons, takes his two daughters hostage. And following the timeworn patterns, he makes a series of women pay the price of his blunder. To his credit, he responds to the voice of the oracle, but it is too late. Antigone dies under his imprisonment; his son dies at the loss of Antigone; his wife dies at the loss of all that is precious to her.

Few moments in mythology have so tragically wounded feminine values.

* See my forthcoming book on the development of male consciousness for the many parallels between Faust and Oedipus.

8

The Continuing Saga

〜∞〜

There are illustrations from mythology and literature that mark the continuing absence of feminine value in Western culture. This one-sided attitude has prevailed almost unchallenged until our own century.

Both Christianity and Judaism held extreme patriarchal views of the nature of humanity. It is a shock to discover that the sixth-century church council at Mâcon (a province in France just north of Lyons) had a long debate on whether women had a soul. When the final count was taken, the decision was affirmative—by one vote! Only a little earlier, St. Augustine had said that women should be given no more power, since they already had so much. Though an oblique tribute to the innate power of women— and femininity—this shows an inability to integrate respect for feminine value into daily human life.

Another tale of femininity lost is the romance of Tristan and Iseult. It originated in the twelfth century, along with the Grail myth, and is fundamental to much of modern thought. The beginning of this story is cold and void of feeling, almost to the point of inhumanity.

King Mark of Cornwall has been aided by his friend, King Rivalen of Lyonesse, in a desperate battle. In return, Mark offers his friend Blanche Fleur, his sister, in marriage. This is the first blow to femininity: she of the white flower is given like a piece of property as political patronage. With femininity so little valued, it is not surprising that the story evolves as one of love failed. Any exchange or beginning that does not give femininity an honored place cannot prosper. As the tale continues, Blanche Fleur learns that her husband has been killed in some masculine enterprise just the day before the birth of her son. In despair at these repeated blows to her dignity and worth, Blanche Fleur names her son Tristan, which means "sorrowful one," and then dies of grief.

The story proceeds from this wrong beginning and perpetuates the error in endless episodes until it ends in the meaningless death of Tristan himself. The low value given femininity at the beginning of the story culminates in the loss of life itself at the end.

The Tristan and Iseult myth still has a profound influence on our collective thought and customs: falling in love as the supreme human experience. Even if one has never heard this story about the power of romantic love, its values reverberate in our deepest unconscious, affecting our attitudes toward marriage, position, power, wealth. Until this illusory quest for the perfect romantic partner is clarified in our collective thought, we cannot make peace with the feminine side of our nature.*

◈

Our next exemplar of the rape of femininity by masculinity is seen in Shakespeare's *Romeo and Juliet*. We find there that little has changed since Creon asserted: "We'll have no woman's law here, while I live." There shall be no love while exclusive masculine values are in power. Power is often exercised at the expense of love, so love perishes.

Romeo and Juliet begins with the feud of two households, the Montagues and Capulets. The prevailing patriarchal values of power, domain, prestige, and authority have set the two aristocratic families against each other. Aristocracy, which should be the basis for high consciousness, is too often marked by the bitterest feuds and power struggles.

The two young lovers, each representing one of the opposing households, have the burden of healing this rift. The prologue sets the archetypal scene:

Two households, both alike in dignity,
    In fair Verona, where we lay our scene,
From ancient grudge break to new mutiny,

* See my book *We* for an elaboration of the Tristan and Iseult theme.

The Continuing Saga

Where civil blood makes civil hands unclean.
From forth the fatal loins of these two foes
    A pair of star-cross'd lovers take their life;
Whose misadventur'd piteous overthrows
    Do with their death bury their parents' strife.
The fearful passage of their death-mark'd love,
    And the continuance of their parents' rage,
Which, but their children's end,
    nought could remove,
    Is now the two hours' traffic of our stage;
The which if you with patient ears attend,
    What here shall miss,
        our toil shall strive to mend.

As Romeo and Juliet approach each other in gentle love, they are surrounded by the tide of a thousand years of power, ownership, and the dominance of the patriarchal world. The young Mercutio mouths vile speeches that advise Romeo to take his pleasure and forget about any cost or commitment.

The ape is dead, and I must conjure him.
I conjure thee by Rosaline's bright eyes,
By her high forehead and her scarlet lip,
By her fine foot, straight leg,
    and quivering thigh,
And the demesnes that there adjacent lie,
That in thy likeness thou appear to us!

Mercutio would have us think that love is nothing but a "quivering thigh, and the demesnes that there

49

THE FEMININE IN WESTERN CULTURE

adjacent lie." Shakespeare in his genius placed this
degrading speech right before Romeo's declaration to
Juliet, the greatest profession of love ever written.

Romeo says of Mercutio: "A gentleman, nurse, that
loves to hear himself talk, and will speak more in a
minute than he will stand to in a month." Juliet's
nurse is an older and feminine voice of the same per-
suasion. She advises her lady to go along with her
parents' plan to make an advantageous marriage to
Paris, whom Juliet loathes. The nurse tells Juliet it is
wise to marry as ordered and to meet her beloved
Romeo in private for her pleasure.

> Well, you have made a simple choice; you know
> not how to choose a man. Romeo! no, not he.
> Though his face be better than any man's, yet his
> leg excels all men's; and for a hand, and a foot,
> and a body, though they be not to be talk'd on,
> yet they are past compare. He is not the flower of
> courtesy, but, I'll warrant him, as gentle as a
> lamb. Go thy ways, wench; serve God.

Juliet should make the political marriage and forget
her feelings: "serve God," the nurse advises. She
makes blasphemy of Juliet's love of Romeo, "and for
a hand, and a foot, and a body, though they be not to
be talk'd on." She reports: "Your love says, like an
honest gentleman, and a courteous, and a kind, and
a handsome, and, I warrant, a virtuous—" this of
Paris, the man Juliet's parents demand she marry. In

the nurse's mentality, devotion is only a leg, a hand, a foot, and a body, while expediency is everything. This is not bawdy speech; it is the murder of everything feminine.

If one ever doubted that the divine feminine (in this case, love and devotion) can be injured as much by woman as by man, here is the proof. From the mouth of a woman we hear the worst blasphemy of all—though Mercutio is a close second.

The play makes its dark way. Romeo and Juliet have taken their love to Friar Laurence, and in his hands another death blow is given to femininity. If the priest, who is to represent love and devotion, had been true, he would have honored the love between the two. But he bows to the prevailing political pressure and tries a devious way to accomplish what, to his small credit, he sees as just. He instructs Juliet to take a potion and sleep a feigned death, so that Romeo may rescue her from her tomb and take her to a land where their love will be safe. But another player fails in his role and, fearful of the plague, does not get the necessary instructions to Romeo. Romeo arrives at the tomb of Juliet uninformed and fails his love by his own suicide. Juliet awakens, not to her lover, but to his corpse. She then commits suicide, which is her failure of love.

This archetypal drama lays out the psychological condition of Europe as Shakespeare saw it. Everyone involved fails to protect the feminine value that could have healed the split between the two warring families. First, the noble families have fallen into the medieval heresy of power enmity. Then a friend, Mercutio, advises Romeo to follow a hedonistic philosophy. Even the nurse—a woman, who should be closer to feminine values—advises duplicity. The priest fails to defend the value of love, which should have been his first concern. A courier fails to carry his message because of fear. Least culpable, but in the same lineage of values, the two lovers fail each other.

Throughout the whole story, however, is sounded the note of redemption; the two noble houses at last make peace, ending their feud over the funeral of the two lovers. This play is Shakespeare's appraisal of the interplay of a power-mad masculinity and a submerged femininity, the order of his day.*

Our attitudes toward femininity are so deeply ingrained in our thought and language over three or four millennia that we lose sight of our question. Even to question is masculine and can move the inquiry in the wrong direction.

---

* All quotations are from the Complete Works of Shakespeare, Abbey Library.

2

The Feminine in
Hindu Mythology

9

A Different Attitude

Exploration of another culture can enable us to see more clearly how not to sacrifice human warmth and grace.

An Indian story that parallels the Oedipal myth reveals quite a different attitude toward femininity. Again, it is myth that provides psychological insight into a cultural attitude. The Hindu sacred scripture the *Mahabharata* dates from about the same period as our Old and New Testaments; it is three times their combined length. A small segment of the *Mahabharata*, the story of Nala and Damayanti, offers us another perspective on the balance between masculine and feminine values. The characters in the *Mahabharata* manage to safeguard the principle of femininity and relatedness somewhat better than our Western heroes do.

A word of caution: I do not present this Eastern culture as superior to our own; but we can learn about the feminine from it. Failure to develop technologically pushed Indian society toward economic and environmental crisis. But it has maintained a valuation of human relations that greatly surpasses that of Western society.

Traditional India refused to adopt any technology that, directly or indirectly, would endanger human relationships and feminine values. Assembly-line techniques, relocation of families to cities, breaking of family ties by sending the wage earner to a distant workplace—such practices were viewed as too dangerous. To safeguard the feminine values, India sacrificed industrial progress. No traditional Indian would challenge this choice.

In Western culture, we encouraged industrialization but failed to safeguard our relationships, both among ourselves and with the world around us. As a result, we are in great danger of destroying relational life, just as India is in danger of being engulfed by poverty and famine. The threat to the Indians' sense of relatedness grows as they abandon their traditional ways and adopt Western attitudes. The horror stories one hears of the breakdown of relationships in modern India often seem attributable to their espousal of Western ways.

History will have to provide a verdict on who has served humanity better—the materialistic West or the relationship-oriented East. Probably the only intelligent verdict will approve that endeavor which serves both masculine and feminine values and safeguards the value of each.

10

The Story of Damayanti

∽∾∽

The tale of Nala and Damayanti deserves to be approached with some reverence. As myth, this story inevitably speaks of the interior psychological condition of the culture that produced it. Tales of kings and queens, gods and demons, are the time-honored way of examining psychological characteristics and patterns of human behavior. It is not possible to reproduce the magnificence of the story's archaic language, but a segment from a nineteenth-century English translation is appended at the end of this book as an indicator of its timeless beauty.

Once there was a king who was the very flower of virtue but had one glaring fault: he could not withstand the urge to gamble. He was so blinded by this one passion that he was easily beguiled into a gambling game, and with equal ease he could be cheated. He finally lost his kingdom and was exiled to the forest in poverty. His son, Nala, took the throne, and with his wisdom and strength restored the kingdom to its power.

Now, a neighboring king had a daughter approaching marriageable age, who knew no equal in beauty and nobility. Heralds and courtiers took it upon themselves to whisper of Damayanti's virtues. Soon the talk linked the pair, Damayanti and Nala, in excellence. It is not strange that the two came to love each other as if destined by fate, though they had never seen each other in human form. The matter seemed impossible since Nala could not have audience with her. But one day Nala, by chance, caught a golden swan, who bargained for his freedom by promising to court Damayanti for him.

Damayanti's father has announced a contest—a Swayamvara—for his daughter's suitors. The gods, even Indra himself, the ruling deity of all India, enter the competition. Indra finds Nala on the road traveling to enter the contest, and instructs him to court Damayanti on the god's behalf. Nala, in a terrible dilemma between his loyalty to the god and to his own heart, openly courts Damayanti for Indra but quietly declares his own love. Damayanti reveals her love for Nala and decides she will choose Nala publicly at the festival.

The critical moment arrives: the contenders are seated in a circle, and she is to choose. But all look like gods in her eyes! What is she to do? Someone whispers to her that the one human present, Nala, can be recognized because he is obliged to blink his eyes occasionally. Damayanti finds Nala in this way and announces her choice of suitor. The gods, more generous than humans, each give a blessing to the young couple.

All is not well, however. Kali, the god of wrath and destruction, hears that a mere mortal has chosen a human over a god as her consort. Kali declares his wrath, but he has to wait twelve years before he finds a vulnerable point in Nala's character. One day Nala forgets to wash his feet before praying, and Kali gains control over him. This may seem a tiny matter to a Westerner, but any breach of form is thought to be dangerous in India. Preying upon Nala's ancestry, Kali inflames him with an insane need to gamble.

Though his friends counsel him and try to protect him, Nala gambles away the whole kingdom, even down to Damayanti's clothing. She is left with one small cloth for a sari, he with nothing. Nala can do nothing now but depart for the forest with Damayanti and take up the life of an ascetic beggar.

Nala falls into depravity and steals half of Damayanti's modest clothing while she sleeps. He now will have something to wager at his gambling ventures. He loses even this last possession. In terrible shame, he leaves Damayanti, still asleep.

Awakening, Damayanti is inconsolable in her loneliness and loss. She falls into the coils of a giant serpent, but a youth rescues her. She wanders for three days and is told by a band of ascetics that she will soon find her husband, freed from his dice madness and restored to his royal dignity. The ascetics vanish; they have only been a vision.

Damayanti joins a band of merchants who are on their way to Suvahu, the City of Truth. They camp by a lotus lake. In the middle of the night, a herd of wild elephants destroys their camp in indignation at what man has done in taming their brothers. Damayanti then travels alone to the City of Truth, where the queen recognizes her and offers her protection.

Nala has fared little better. He sees a forest on fire and hears Naga, the world serpent, cry from the fire, begging for help. Nala rescues the serpent, but his reward is to be bitten. Naga explains that this bite is the only cure for Nala's dice madness but that Nala will pay for his cure by losing his youth and beauty and grace. Nala, transformed, goes to the City of Truth to exchange his skill at horsemanship for skill at dice.

Damayanti is rescued from the City of Truth by her parents and brought home. Her parents set about to find Nala by a ruse: they announce another Swayamvara for Damayanti. Nala, hearing of this, is in agony. He is working for a man who plans to compete at the Swayamvara. The master asks him to manage the horses and is so impressed by Nala's fine horsemanship that he offers to trade his own skill at dice for

Nala's skill with horses. Nala will now be enabled to purge himself of his madness.

At the Swayamvara, Nala, managing the horses, makes sounds that are uniquely his own. Damayanti recognizes Nala by ear, though not yet by sight. With Damayanti's touch, Nala is restored to his kingly status.

11

Two Love Stories

It is instructive while on our journey through mythology to sample two other short love stories in the *Mahabharata*. They underscore the potency of love and human relatedness as central to Hindu life. In both stories, the main character is a woman, Shakuntalal and Savitri by name.

SHAKUNTALAL AND THE RING

Shakuntalal is the foster daughter of a sage who lives in a simple ashram in the forest. One day, the king comes hunting and finds her picking flowers in the forest. They of course fall in love immediately. They are married, and the king gives Shakuntalal a ring that bears his seal. He leaves to take up his kingly duties, telling Shakuntalal to come to him as soon as possible. The ring will allow her into his court. The sage, her foster father, having been away, returns to discover Shakuntalal is pregnant. He rejoices in her marriage to the king and promises to help her depart when the child is old enough to travel safely. But while Shakuntalal's father was away, another sage came to visit. So caught up in her love for the king was she that she slighted the sage, forgetting the formalities due a visiting yogi. He cursed her, saying that the person she was so distracted by would forget her. She pleaded with him and he modified the curse, promising that if the man saw the ring she was wearing, he would remember her. Alas, she loses the ring on the trip to the king. Surely he will forget her.

Shakuntalal expresses her fury and anguish over being forgotten. Her monologue in court about the irresponsibility of hankering men, written by Kalidasa, India's greatest playwright, is a heroic plea for the dominance of feminine values in the world: stability, comfort, relatedness, and simple love.

Shakuntalal is taken up by the gods to live in heaven, while the king ponders that strange course of events, this "something" which he has forgotten. Finally, a fisherman finds the ring with the royal seal in a lake and brings it to the king, who then remembers all. Searching for Shakuntalal, he finds her and their son on a heavenly mountain, and all are reunited.

SAVITRI IN THE FOREST

Savitri is the feminine form of one of the many words for the sun in Sanskrit. A childless king and queen, having performed a great sacrifice to the sun, are rewarded with a wonderful daughter. Savitri grows into such a splendid woman that no man dares approach her for marriage. So her father suggests that she take a chariot and retinue into the world to seek a husband.

This she does. After long travels throughout the wonderful land of India, she glimpses at the edge of the forest a beautiful youth. In that instant her life changes. Satyavan is the son of a king exiled to the simple life of a forest ascetic because, having become blind, he could not perform his royal duties.

Savitri returns to her father's kingdom to tell her parents of the choice she has made. Narada, the divine messenger and musician, appears to inform the gathered court that Savitri has chosen perfectly. But there is one problem: Satyavan will die a year from the day they are married. The queen is distraught and pleads with Savitri to reconsider. But Savitri will not, for she has made her choice. The marriage is performed, and Savitri goes to the forest to live with her husband and his parents. She serves them well, and they all love her. She remains beautiful and gracious, though life in the forest is difficult.

As the day of Satyavan's death approaches, Savitri begins a fast to gain inner strength. The fateful day arrives, and she requests that he take her with him to cut wood for the fire. He agrees. Satyavan dies during a stroke of the ax.

Death approaches to take his soul while Savitri

holds Satyavan's head in her lap. She follows Death unrelentingly into the infernal realm, and in order to get her to leave them, Death offers several boons from which Savitri can choose: sight for her blind father-in-law, the return of the king to his rightful place, a hundred children for herself. His admiration for Savitri causes Death to forget that in order for her to have children, Satyavan must reside on earth. Death releases Satyavan's soul. Savitri has conquered death through love.

REFLECTIONS

In both these beautiful stories, and in our main story as well, it is the strength of the feminine, the woman as hero, that is the redeeming factor. In all of them, the men somehow cannot provide the focus of femininity to complement their external strength. A divisive crisis is thus produced, which only feminine heroism can resolve.

Surprisingly, Western tradition offers three stories that, in their tragic outcome, exactly invert the three stories from the *Mahabharata*. The tale of Orpheus and Eurydice is an inversion of the quest of Savitri. A male figure uses his feminine strength, represented by music, to reach hell and convince Pluto to release his woman. But his femininity cannot sustain itself to the end, and he fails. Medea's problem with Jason is analogous to Shakuntalal's with her king. But Medea kills her two sons to exact revenge, and love is lost.

Romeo and Juliet are teenage lovers, like Nala and Damayanti. But Juliet is victimized by a well-meaning but insufficient priest, and the lovers die.

All mythology presents much the same theme—the interaction between archetypal figures and/or humans. We spend most of our personal lives in the horizontal interplay of opposing forces, the perpetual tug-of-war between personal events as they are and events as we would like them to be. This generates human energy and is the source of what we do as humans. We may call it the drama of life. But there is another, vertical, interplay, which is the drama of levels, the interaction of gods and people. This is the realm of mythology, a whole level of drama above the usual human interplay. Our term for this dimension of experience is fate.

Fate plays an equally powerful role in the Oedipus myth and in our Hindu stories. Oedipus was assigned a fate, which was announced long before he was born, and we cannot fault him for his heritage. No less is fate represented in the myth of Nala and Damayanti, where circumstances bring them together and where the gods intercede and wish to supersede human behavior. Nothing but mythology and fate is strong enough to cope with the dilemma of Nala and Damayanti when they want to marry, but the gods want Damayanti for themselves. Ordinary human intelligence, designed to work with the human interplay of likes and dislikes, good and evil, cannot deal with this vertical cleavage, and the story must run its fateful course to find a solution.

We cannot be charged for fate, for it is not of our making; but the manner in which we proceed with that fate is our responsibility. Though the story has escaped from human dimensions when it makes its vertical cleavage, still, it is the actions—noble or ignoble—of the humans that bring the story to a noble or disastrous end. Oedipus proved the power of human nobility; Creon brought disaster down upon himself and the House of Thebes. Oedipus acted in a human and related way within his fate; Creon played power games and destroyed everything within his range. One brought the greatest flowering of culture ever recorded in history—the golden age of Athens; the other set a pattern of dysfunctional relationships that is still operating today. It is this human action that catches our attention in both myths. The nobility or disaster of the story is determined by that action.

First, it is saddening to see how badly men act in both the Greek and the Hindu myths. But the women stand firm in the East Indian myth, as they are unable to do in the Greek myth. This theme of the interplay of masculine and feminine elements challenges each of us. We can learn from it. If the feminine element will hold firm, the fateful story then can have a positive relational outcome. No matter what fate befalls us—even a very dark one—we will be safe if the feminine can hold.

Our East Indian story tells of the impact of the gods upon human life as individuals are torn from the ordinary paths of conventional behavior. From the very beginning, the masculine element is swallowed up by its shadowy side—dice playing. Gambling can be perceived as a deeply ingrained dimension of masculine behavior. Nala's father loses his kingdom because he cannot overcome his urge to gamble. The gods know exactly where to touch Nala to punish him for his interference in their realm. To see this behavior in our own time, just listen to a modern mother trying to dissuade her son from entering a dangerous motorcycle competition. A friend called the other day to say that she was trying to maintain her composure that afternoon while her son went skydiving. Dice playing has its equivalents in various eras.

Nala and Damayanti are following a normal course of human life when the gods intercede—a sure sign that an evolution is imminent. Nala is obliged to bear the tension of being split between his loyalty to the gods and his own wishes for Damayanti. When such a split takes place, it can be healed only by heroic action. Nala finally performs such action and brings healing. Damayanti remains firm in her loyalty, devotion, and insight and makes it possible for Nala to follow his heroic path. This is equally heroism, in its feminine aspect.

Damayanti is the key figure of the story, and it is her strength and wisdom that bring it to a happy conclusion. First, she has the capacity to endure. She waits in her father's house until her prince finds her. But next she chooses—that is, she maintains a realistic human perspective when she is offered a god as a husband. This is extremely important and represents a moment in femininity (and a moment in a woman's life) when a woman stays rooted in her humanity. She avoids the romantic fantasy of a god as a lover. This requires a finely tuned ability to make psychological and emotional distinctions. She is aware of the human characteristic of blinking the eyes, something not required of the gods. She is aware of limits and chooses the limited human, who needs to blink his eyes, over the divine, which would be timeless and immortal. She is capable of seeing that the human condition is preferable to the divine at a particular point in her life.

Then Damayanti is required to wait and endure for what must seem endless time. She watches her man, Nala, pursue his mad folly of gambling, and she remains loyal to him. If this were taken literally, it would appear that a woman must follow a man slavishly, no matter how nonsensical his activities. But this is a discussion about interior masculinity and femininity and is not meant to be taken literally. It is a total misunderstanding of psychological reality when a society or culture sustains a patriarchal dictum that woman is to serve man unquestioningly. Femininity may serve masculinity, but this must be understood as an interior dynamic and not as an external, relational convention. It is the very essence of femininity to know when to act from a center of relatedness and when to be quiet and endure. No man can tell a woman which of these responses is appropriate at a particular moment, but there is a center of feminine wisdom that can guide a woman unerringly.

Damayanti never departs from her relatedness: At each moment of the story, it is the prevailing principle of her life. When she uses her masculine quality of differentiation, she does so in the service of her genius for relatedness. It is her capacity to act when required and to endure when that is appropriate that produces the redemptive power.

Near the end of the story, Damayanti must recognize Nala in the form of an unattractive old man. She does this by sound, the only characteristic from the past that Nala has retained. But it is enough, and she makes the correct identification. Women in their relationships with men often feel that the men disappear psychologically and emotionally. This ability to identify one small sign of a man's true nature and connect with it can help him toward wholeness.

The end of the story is a great triumph and is largely the result of Damayanti's wisdom. She holds firm, is strong or quiet, acts or is still, remaining connected to her feminine wisdom, and she brings the story to its very Indian conclusion. This and other Indian stories are the truest examples I know of the redemptive power of femininity. If femininity remains clear and strong, it provides the wisdom and power to thwart a negative movement of fate.

3

What Does Woman
Really Want?

12

Femininity Lost

The timeless ingredients of the soul can never be forced into subjection for long. The feminine, which had been placed in an inferior role by both the Greek and the Hebrew worlds, made a dramatic and powerful bid for a place in the sun of consciousness in the twelfth century. An explosion, a tidal wave of energy, rose up out of the collective unconscious and was immediately repressed, but it still reverberates in our unconscious to this day.* Western man, especially in France, was seized by an adoration of the lofty nature of femininity and devised a particularly tender expression of it. Chivalry, courtliness (we still honor this by our word "courtesy," which has its root in "court"), the troubadours, the minnesingers, and the

---

* Carl Jung describes the underpinning of mankind, the world soul, that which we all share in common, as the "collective unconscious." This often erupts as a product of the soul of mankind in a particular age, such as the Renaissance, the Gothic period, the Age of Enlightenment.

gottesingers sprang up as from a parched land after a rainfall. Devotion to women became the order of the day. A young man would travel from one court to another, lute in hand, to pay court to ladies who had caught his heart. He would sing love songs to a fair lady, perhaps receive a talisman from her hands, and when this subtle courtship was completed, he would wander off and find another fair lady for his devotion. This was an age when the ideal and mundane dimensions of life were fracturing into painful opposites, and that fracture was apparent in the art of courtly love. Conventions did not allow the couple to express their devotion physically. A knight would lay siege to a lady's heart, but the connection was not to be tested by their entering into a practical human relationship. It was the divine dimension of love that flowered, without the encumbrance of practicality. A poem by Chrétien de Troyes tells the plaintive story of courtly love:

> From all ills mine differs;
> It pleasures me;
>   I rejoice in it;
> My illness is what
>   I want
> And my pain is my health!
> I don't see, then,
>   of what I complain,
> For my illness comes to
>   me of my own will;

It is my own wish
    that becomes my ill,
But I find so much
    pleasure in wishing thus
That I suffer
    agreeably,
And so much
    joy within my pain
That I am sick
    with delight.

One can understand this best by remembering that it happened against the backdrop of the Gothic age. In the Gothic ideal, matter is allowed only the most tenuous possible basis, from which the spirit can soar. Gothic architecture asks stone to do almost more than stone is able to bear. A Gothic building is designed on the basic proportions of five units of height to one unit of width. The architects managed to form stone into this proportion, and those great buildings still stand, for our edification. But the human soul, perhaps better informed than the human intellect, does not bear this imbalance of height over breadth.

For some fifty years of heady romance, chivalry reigned supreme in the courts of Europe. Femininity was served, perhaps with a nobility never seen before or since; but it was so narrow and fragile an ideal that it fell of its own lack of substance. The church found this very feminine outpouring of the human soul much too one-sided and banished the song of the troubadour as heresy. This was the Albigensian heresy, so called because the new chivalric cult centered around the southern French town of Albi.

Once seen and experienced, though, such a flowering cannot be entirely forgotten, and chivalry has kept a small corner of our attention from that day until now. I went to my safe-deposit box the other day and a woman bank employee took me into the vault. When it was time to leave, I refused to go before her, and in the impasse I said, "Chivalry is not entirely dead." There was a smile: softness and warmth filled even that modern stainless-steel vault. So the feminine has maintained a tenuous thread in our customs since that time of lutes and troubadours. In a narrow band of human experience, power can give way to love. So femininity made a bold bid for human dignity, but its form was too slender and ethereal to hold. It left the bright—though admittedly artificial—light of the French age of chivalry and went underground again.

Even before its masculine repression and overpowering of the feminine in this specific historical moment, the attitude of the Church was clear. The Christian Church has lived with a trinitarian view of reality for most of its theological life. From a masculine point of view, this has been quite satisfactory, as it makes for an orderly, well-formed, predictable attitude. In other words, it fits well into a masculine mentality. The inevitable consequence of a trinitarian viewpoint is the exclusion of the feminine element. But it follows us, demanding to be included in our life and given a place of dignity.

Jung pointed out that Western Christianity unconsciously made its cross, the pictorial representation of its theology, with one arm longer than the other. Since Western Christianity gave less than its deserved place to matter and femininity, it was compelled to compensate for this and extended the cross's bottom arm, yielding a distorted mandala as its central symbol. The Eastern branches of Christianity remained less caught in the heresy of denying the divinity of matter and femininity, and their cross was given equal arms. One can sense even today that the Greeks honor the earthly dimensions of life more than we do. Their cross is eloquent testimony of this.

INVITING THE SHADOW TO DINNER

We repeat the obvious in saying that feminine energy is and has been an excluded element in Western culture. But what becomes even more complex for human growth and understanding is that an excluded element often seems like a "dark" or "shadow" energy before it is reintegrated. Jung once observed that if you are pursued by a lion in your dream (pursuit being a favorite way for dreams to present an excluded element), what are you to do? Why, turn around, of course, and say to the lion, "Please, will you be so kind as to eat me?" Then the lion explains that he is the emissary of God and asks why you have made it so hard for him to bring the gift of God.

"Rancid" is the eloquent term the psychologist Marie Louise von Franz uses for a degraded quality denied its place in the sun. A quarter of our nature was denied dignity or consciousness and went rancid. It is extremely important to understand that the misuse or misplacing of the quality is the danger, not the quality itself. We make this psychological and spiritual mistake repeatedly in our personal and cultural lives.

When an excluded element is restored to dignity and awarded its true value, it quickly becomes a positive and creative element. One day I was at a Hollywood recording studio with my harpsichord, painfully aware of the unfeeling, harsh, competitive atmosphere of that industry. It seems that feeling becomes particularly fragile where art becomes industry. Employing my usual device of transparency to protect myself, I was delighted to hear a gentle, well-modulated English voice behind me. A pent-up sum of warmth and appreciation flooded into my consciousness, and I said, "What a very beautiful voice you have!" The young lady addressed, caught unaware, burst into tears and fled. I have never seen her since, but I suspect that neither of us will ever forget the other. Feeling and femininity in a harsh environment carry overwhelming power. One remembers this for a lifetime, even when it is a glance from a stranger.

It is the most profound task of our age to give the sensuous and feminine elements this dignity, even in small ways, in order to restore them to their true creativeness. Who knows how many of our symptoms—both personal and collective—will turn bright if we can give them dignity?

Jung and Von Franz found in the dreams of modern people the universal theme of moving "from three to four." This compelling and prevalent dream motif signals the loss of an essential element, the missing fourth, and its attempt to return to the personal and cultural lives of Western humanity.

Contrastingly, this "dark fourth" occupies a place of dignity and beauty in Indian theology. There is a trinity of gods—Brahma, the creator; Vishnu, the sustainer; and Siva, the destroyer (who removes old forms to make way for new). These gods are portrayed as predominantly masculine, though they have feminine counterparts. The great joy of the Indian conception of this issue is that the fourth, taking the place of our Christian devil, is Krishna, the dancing god, who is so full of life and joy and exuberance that he brings happiness to anyone near him. He has sixteen thousand wives, sports with the Gopis (milkmaids), plays his flute to the eternal delight of the world, and generally brings a bright sensuousness wherever he goes. What a delight to find the elements that we call satanic treated in so happy and joyous a way!

Krishna and Christ bear many characteristics in common, beginning with their names. Krishna was born into a hostile land, where the reigning tyrant decreed that all children under a certain age should be killed so that the new incarnation would not supplant the tyrannical old king. Krishna was painted blue to protect him from the soldiers, whose evil eyes were unable to see that color. Thus Krishna is generally portrayed as blue, which indicates his high spirituality. His sky color protects him from the old order.

In a country where the feminine-sensuous is given so joyous a role, you can expect a different set of attitudes. Traditional India is a place where femininity and the sensuous dimensions of life are awarded the dignity and nobility they deserve.

THE ULTIMATE YEARNING

The loss of feminine energy, with its warm vitality, is not difficult to document. It is evident in our culture's mythic traditions, in our linguistic poverty, in our lack of feeling for human relationships, and finally in our hunger for meaning. Meaning is the realm of the feminine. Without secure femininity in our interior psychological world, no contentment or meaning is possible. We have alienated ourselves from this fact of our being. We burden ourselves with a hundred different demands or expectations, which disguise our simple need to be and to have meaning. Still, we have experienced moments of peace, which remind us of the essential quality of meaning. The simplest meal is worth remembering for a lifetime if it is the carrier of meaning and human connection.

13

Femininity Regained

ภฒ

Femininity is so basic and fundamental a part of human personality that it cannot be disregarded for long. It may be set aside for a period of time, so that masculinity may solidify the patriarchal values of law, order, form, and science. It is unlikely that these values can be established and rooted unless they are given exclusive rights to the center of the stage of evolution, as has been the case for the last three thousand years. But the feminine will return and take its rightful place as soon as the masculine evolution is secure. Some bright and warm examples of this return are to be seen in our age. Probably humanity has never been in so rich a position as now; a golden age of mechanical power is available, and a new age of feminine values is possible. To establish the basis for leisure, which the modern world offers great numbers of people, has been a noble accomplishment. Adding the feminine insights to a conscious mentality is our next step. As truly modern people, we are at the crest of a wave where the best of both worlds can be achieved if we are wise enough to escape the modern prejudice of one-sidedness. To fail in this wisdom is to invite the worst of both worlds, which would set us back into the Dark Ages.

The Roman Catholic Church is attempting in its own way to reintegrate the feminine dimension in its theology and in Catholic life. In 1950, a significant milestone was reached with the doctrine of the bodily assumption of the Virgin Mary, an audacious statement that joined the Virgin Mary in her physical body to the all-male trinity. Jung, jubilant at this great evolutionary advance, commented that it marked the greatest moment in Church history since the Reformation. For a body as traditionally conservative as the Catholic Church to honor the new feminine dimensions is indeed a great moment in the history of civilization. Marian Year has come and gone with little apparent effect; but the doctrine is there and is working its way into the exclusive masculine theology of the trinity.

A profound lesson about the way that feminine energy can be returned to modern life is illustrated by one of the legends of King Arthur. Again we return to the mythic dimension of life to learn about our interior psychological dynamics. In general, the Arthurian stories chronicle the new idea of chivalry and nobility, but they recount only a partial delivery of femininity from its bondage. One story, though, is far in advance of its time (or are we so far behind in our comprehension?), alluding to a transformation of darkness into light. It is the story of Arthur and the puzzling question: "What does woman really want?"

King Arthur, in his youth, was caught poaching in the forests of the neighboring kingdom and was caught by its king. He might well have been killed immediately, for that was the punishment for transgressing the laws of property and ownership. But the neighboring king was touched by Arthur's youth and winsome character. He offered Arthur freedom if he could find the answer to a very difficult question within one year. The question? What does woman really want? This would stagger the wisest of men and seemed insurmountable for the youth. But it was better than hanging, so Arthur returned home and began questioning everyone he could find. Harlot and nun, princess and queen, wise man and court fool—all were approached, but none could give a convincing answer. Each advised, however, that there was one who would know, the old witch. The cost would be high, for it was proverbial in the realm that the old witch charged ruinous prices for her services.

The last day of the year arrived, and Arthur finally was driven to consult the hag. She agreed to provide an answer that would satisfy, but the price had to be discussed first. And her price was marriage to Gawain, the noblest knight of the Round Table and Arthur's closest friend. Arthur gazed at the old witch in horror: she was ugly, had but one tooth, gave forth a stench that would sicken a goat, made obscene sounds, and was humpbacked—the most loathsome creature he had ever encountered. Arthur quailed at the prospect of asking his lifelong friend to assume this terrible burden for him. But Gawain, hearing of the bargain, asserted that this was not too much to offer for the life of his companion and the preservation of the Round Table.

The wedding was announced, and the old hag gave of her infernal wisdom: What does woman really want? She wants sovereignty over her own life! Everyone knew on the instant of hearing this that great feminine wisdom had been spoken and King Arthur would be safe. The neighboring ruler did, indeed, give Arthur his freedom when he heard the answer.

But the wedding! All the court was there, and none was more torn between relief and distress than Arthur himself. Gawain was courteous, gentle, and respectful; the old witch exhibited her worst manners, wolfed the food from her plate without aid of utensils, emitted hideous noises and smells. Never before or since had the court of Arthur been subject to such a strain. But courtesy prevailed, and the wedding was accomplished.

Over the wedding night we shall draw a curtain of circumspection, except for one astonishing moment. When Gawain was prepared for the wedding bed and waiting for his bride to join him, she appeared as the loveliest maiden a man could ever wish to see! Gawain in his amazement asked what had happened.

The maiden replied that because Gawain had been courteous to her, she would show him her hideous aspect half of the time and her gracious aspect the other half of the time: which did he choose for the day and which for the night? This was a cruel question to put before a man, and Gawain made rapid calculations. Did he want a lovely maiden to show forth during the day, when all of his friends could see, and a hideous hag at night in the privacy of their chamber; or did he want a hag during the day and a maiden in the intimate moments of their life? The noble Gawain replied that he would let his bride choose for herself. At this, she announced that she would be fair damsel to him both day and night, since he had given her respect and sovereignty over her own life.

If femininity has been driven into its hideous mode, the best that a man can do is maintain respect and courtesy. This is the magic of transformation, which will restore femininity gone dark more quickly to its true beauty than any other means. This story about the dynamic of interior feminine energy is as important for men attempting to relate to their inner feminine side as it is for women trying to live out of their core identity. And it is a principle that should not be lost on external male-female relationships.

I recently found an example of femininity regained in an unlikely place. In James Joyce's *Ulysses*, there is a high moment of feeling and redemption. The novel is so difficult and hard to bear that parts of it would sicken a goat. The story goes and goes and goes through the bankruptcy of turn-of-the-century Dublin, the hypocrisy of the Church, corrupt city officials, a school system that would spawn nightmares for future generations, failure of friendship and trust. The feminine principle of life has been so destroyed that even the women of the story have lost their way. Our hero is so worn down by his despair that he sees no way out. But Joyce, certainly one of the geniuses of the modern world, finds redemption of all this chaos in the most unlikely place. He puts one of the greatest affirmations of life ever written in a monologue delivered by an unattractive woman on the very last pages of the novel. That statement is the more powerful for being placed in so dismal a setting. I had to try several times before I survived reading the novel to its end. But the reward for persistence was a glorious affirmation of life that could be located only in a feminine soul. One sees our bankrupt age redeemed by the genius of a modern prophet.

Molly Bloom, the wife of an unattractive character who does little but flow with the tide of the day, lies in bed, drifting off into a reverie. She reviews the little things of her life, things of small consequence; but a miracle happens on the stage of her simple feminine nature. She punctuates her endless sentence of reverie with the word "yes" more and more frequently, until finally that endless sentence is a great cry of hope and affirmation and belief in life. The overpowering reiteration of "yes" redeems everything that surrounds it and makes a work of art out of tawdry things that represent despair to a lesser eye. Molly Bloom redeems life—something only the feminine can accomplish in a bankrupt masculine world.

. . . ah yes I know them well who was the first person in the universe before there was anybody that made it all who ah that they dont know neither do I so there you are they might as well try to stop the sun from rising tomorrow the sun shines for you he said the day we were lying among the rhododendrons on Howth head in the grey tweed suit and his straw hat the day I got him to propose to me yes first I gave him the bit of seedcake out of my mouth and it was leap-year like now yes 16 years ago my God after that long kiss I near lost my breath yes he said I was a flower of the mountain yes so we are flowers all a womans body yes that was one true thing he said in his life and the sun shines for you today yes that was why I liked him because I saw he understood or felt what a woman is and I knew I could always get round him and I gave him all the pleasure I could leading him on till he asked me to say yes and I wouldnt answer first only looked out over the sea and the sky I was thinking of so many things he didnt know of Mulvey and Mr Stanhope and Hester and father and old captain Groves and the sailors playing all birds fly and I say stoop and washing up dishes they called it on the pier and the sentry in front of the governors house with the thing round his white helmet poor devil half roasted

and the Spanish girls laughing in their shawls
and their tall combs and the auctions in the
morning the Greeks and the jews and the Arabs
and the devil knows who else from all the ends
of Europe and Duke street and the fowl market
all clucking outside Larby Sharons and the poor
donkeys slipping half asleep and the vague fel-
lows in the cloaks asleep in the shade on the
steps and the big wheels of the carts of the bulls
and the old castle thousands of years old yes and
those handsome Moors all in white and turbans
like kings asking you to sit down in their little bit
of a shop and Ronda with the old windows of
the posadas glancing eyes a lattice hid for her
lover to kiss the iron and the wineshops half
open at night and the castanets and the night we
missed the boat at Algeciras the watchman going
about serene with his lamp and O that awful
deepdown torrent O and the sea the sea crimson
sometimes like fire and the glorious sunsets and
the figtrees in the Alameda gardens yes and all
the queer little streets and pink and blue and
yellow houses and the rosegardens and the
jessamine and geraniums and cactuses and
Gibraltar as a girl where I was a Flower of the
mountain yes when I put the rose in my hair like
the Andalusian girls used or shall I wear a red
yes and how he kissed me under the Moorish
wall and I thought well as well him as another
and then I asked him with my eyes to ask again
yes and then he asked me would I yes to say yes
my mountain flower and first I put my arms
around him yes and drew him down to me so he

89

could feel my breasts all perfume yes and his heart was going like mad and yes I said yes I will Yes.

To turn the tide of at least four thousand years of patriarchy is not to be accomplished in a moment of history. The issues are becoming more clearly defined, and they are affecting every part of our society. We can hope this continues, and it will if we all join the adventurers of the inner landscape on the heroic quest.

14

The Heroic Task

~~~~

The heroic task is different for men and women, even though in this age we would like to blur the distinctions. This blurring is unfortunate, and it indicates a major misunderstanding of the levels of human action. The difficulty lies in the differentiating of levels. The confusion of levels is so commonplace in psychological attitudes that few people consider the subject. Something is true only on the level on which it is appropriate. For example: Mythology is true (sublimely true!) on an inner level, but it makes no sense on a historical level. Maleness is an outer physical attribute of half of humanity; masculinity is an attribute of every human being. It follows from this that one must be exceedingly careful how one applies masculinity or femininity to one's personality. A very powerful law may be formulated from this information: if a woman remains firmly rooted in her femininity, she may make the most excellent use of

masculine characteristics; but if masculine characteristics dominate her basic personality, she will, at best,
be only an imitation male. A man may make excellent
use of femininity to enrich his basic personality; but if
he is dominated by these feminine qualities, he will
be overwhelmed by his moods and irrational behavior. Like fire, our contrasexual capacities make a wonderful servant but a terrible master.

Staying alert to the differences between men and
women, masculinity and femininity, and to psychological levels was graphically illustrated for me during a visit to Canterbury Cathedral in England. I spent
the first of my two days there in awe of that great
Gothic building and its majestic portrayal of Christ on
the cross. I had been engaged in my own analytical
process in London for many weeks, and the symbol-
ism of the Gothic building as Christ on the cross had
been a key part of a large dream. I had learned that
the Gothic age honored the crucifixion of Christ in its
architecture with the choir of the building as his head,
the two transepts as his two arms, the nave as his
body, and the two west towers as his feet. There is no
entrance to the Gothic building in the choir, signifying that there is no access to Christ consciousness by
way of the head. There are entrances at each transept, signifying that it is possible to contact Christ
through the hands; but the official entrance is by way
of the feet, the two west towers. When there is an
official entrance to a Gothic building, it is at one of the
west towers or the central portal in between. Once

every ten years, the Pope knocks at the central door of St. Peter's in Rome to ask admission. Even he must come humbly to the feet of Christ to ask admittance. It is through the most earthy part of our nature that Christ is available. The medieval mind believed that the soul could enter and leave the body only through the soles of the feet. It is for this reason that *soul* and *sole* bear the same significance.

I had been meditating all day on this awesome and humbling fact and experimenting to see what happened to my feelings and intuition when I entered or left the cathedral through a transept and through the west door. The transepts always gave me a sense of asymmetry or one-sidedness. The west door gave me a sense of symmetry and balance. The implications of this in regard to the practical affairs of my life flooded through me. Then an unexpected confirmation came: this great building was indeed the figure of Christ lying outstretched on the cross! But a much greater insight followed: every person I met on the High Street of Canterbury was a living figure of Christ, in flesh and blood! I left the cathedral and spent the rest of my visit to Canterbury walking on the High Street, watching people and being in the presence of the crucifixion enacted in time and space. I still loved the great Gothic building, but it had been superseded by the living space-time drama on the High Street.

This was a profound revelation for me, but the subject was not yet finished. Weeks later, I was telling a friend what had happened to me in Canterbury, and she exclaimed in amazement that exactly the same thing had happened to her there—but in reverse! She had been at home with the human drama on the High Street. But at a profound moment she had discovered that the Gothic cathedral embodied everything she needed to experience and that she no longer needed the street and its teeming life.

This is a profound story of a man discovering the feminine truth of flesh and blood portrayed in time and space, and a woman finding her masculine truth in the abstraction of symbol. God grant that men and women may meet and honor each other as they pass in the middle on their holy journey.

Of course, new attitudes in anything so basic as this subject will be clumsy at first. For example, it is easy to fall into the trap of thinking that to imitate maleness is to acquire masculinity. In the first flush of joy at discovering opera in my teens, I saw an Italian production in which a quartet of voices sang a famous aria. In order to make characters and voices harmonize, the alto voice had to be played as a man. The woman singing the alto role and portraying a man so exaggerated the bravado and the domineering qualities of stereotypical masculinity that I was horrified. Was this what a man looked like through the eyes of a woman? My inquiry into the difference between male and masculine began at that moment. Few things in this world are as ridiculous as an insecure man or woman adopting the stereotypes of his or her role to compensate for the deficit. Equally ridiculous is the practice of women adopting masculine stereotypes to breach the "patriarchal barrier"; or a man adopting the stereotypes of femininity in his effort to grow more sensitive. Neither rings true, and both can create relational and cultural tyrannies.

In her book, *The Wounded Woman*, Linda Schierse Leonard* points out a very important fact about Western mythology: there are no feminine heroes. The lack of feminine heroes in Western mythic literature seems linked to another important and equally startling fact. All the great love stories of India work through to a "successful" conclusion; all the great love stories of the West, on the other hand, are tragic. What this means is that in the West, death is the only means to final union. Unity seems to be conceived in the West as something that can occur only beyond the realm of physical reality. India, however, for all its intense spiritual discipline, cannot conceive of a tragic end to love.

Why might this be so? It is to the element of feminine heroism that we must turn to find the answer. Feminine heroism is what is required of us now, of all of us, men and women. In the divisive strengths of masculinized world culture, we must hold to the basic simplicities that bind us and make us whole. This is now the Great Quest. No longer can we be the conquering (masculine) hero, who defends his terri-

---

* Linda Schierse Leonard. *The Wounded Woman* (Boston: Shambhala Publications, 1982).

tory, his principles, his woman, his rights. We must become the embracing hero, who finds the right place for each relationship in life, who nurtures and protects and comforts so that growth can take place, not in a field of illusions, but in a field of love and wholeness.

This heroism requires all the skill and intelligence, all the strength and courage, of the heroism with which we are more familiar. Perhaps it requires even more. For it is less flamboyant, less fulfilling to the ego, less immediately satisfying to our base instincts. But without it, the prognosis for the future of humankind on this green and dangerous planet is bleak indeed.

We think that love is natural, that it requires no skill, no creativity to maintain. We feel that it is somehow artificial to be polite or kind, to make the effort to learn how to love. There are few attitudes in the history of the race that have had more disastrous repercussions than this.

Yet don't all the great warrior heroes also have their time of training, their apprenticeship, where they learned their martial ways? Can we expect less of love? Does not our new quest, our new heroism, demand at least as much, if not more? Let one of the masters of this heroism, Rainer Maria Rilke, speak for us:

young people, who are beginners in everything, cannot yet know love, they have to learn it. With their whole being, with all their forces, gathered close about their lonely, timid, upward-beating heart, they must learn to love. But learning-time is always a long, secluded time, and so loving, for a long while ahead and far on into life, is solitude, intensified and deepened loneness for him who loves. Love is at first not anything that means merging, giving over, and uniting with another (for what would a union be of something unclarified and individual) to ripen, to become something of himself, to become world, to become world for himself for another's sake; it is a great exacting claim upon him, something that chooses him out and calls him to vast things. Only in this sense, as the task of working at themselves ("to hearken and to hammer day and night"), might young people use the love that is given them.

Perhaps we are all yet beginners in love. As Rilke says later in this beautiful passage: "Merging and surrendering and every kind of communion . . . is the ultimate, is perhaps that for which human lives as yet scarcely suffice."*

So we should not, perhaps, feel too sad about our failures in such a demanding task. Yet it is a task that we must take up in earnest—to restore true femininity to a place of dignity, power, and honor, to learn to love—if our planet and our civilization are to survive much beyond our present era.

* Ranier Maria Rilke, *Letters to a Young Poet* (New York: W. W. Norton, 1934), p. 54.

ᔥ

A FINAL THOUGHT

It has proved much easier to talk of femininity lost than of femininity regained. What we have lost is so painful to us that it is ever present; what we hunger to regain is vague and exists only as inner pain, sadness, and restlessness. But it pursues us constantly. We are only beginning the task of restoring the precious feminine quality of humanity, which is so infinitely valuable to us. Our discontent and our subtle suffering spring from the loss of the feminine values, and we face formidable obstacles in restoring these values. At present we make feeble attempts at gender equality—getting equal remuneration for equal work, getting respect and dignity—name, title, ownership—for specifically feminine things. But a much more subtle task remains: gaining equal time and dignity for those feeling values that are the subtle dimensions of femininity. Leisure, spontaneity, and artistry ask for dignity and respect equal to the time-honored pursuits of money and security. These tasks remain to be done and await our attention.

Appendix

◁◦▷◦◁

The following is a short section of the story of Nala and Damayanti, quoted in detail to convey the archaic beauty of the original. Though it has suffered violation in its translation from Sanskrit to English, some of the original beauty still shines through. I refer the reader to the translated text if you want to sample the poetic beauty of the story.*

And Damana, well-pleased, granted unto the king and his consort a boon in the form of a jewel of a daughter, and three sons possessed of lofty souls and great fame. They were called respectively Damayanti, and Dama and Danta, and illustrious Damana. And the three sons were possessed of every accomplishment and terrible mien and fierce prowess. And the slender-

* *The Mahabharata*, translated by Kishavi Mohan Ganguli (New Delhi: Munshivan Monoharial Publishers, 54 Rani Jhansi Rd. 110055).

waisted Damayanti, in beauty and brightness, in good name and grace and luck, became celebrated all over the world. And on her attaining to age, hundreds of hand-maids, and female slaves, decked in ornament, waited upon her like Sachi herself. And Bhima's daughter of faultless features, decked in every ornament, shone in the midst of her hand-maidens, like the luminous lightning of the clouds. And the large-eyed damsel was possessed of great beauty like that of Sree herself. And neither among the celestials, nor among the Yakshas, nor among men, was anybody possessed of such beauty seen or heard of before. And the beautiful maiden filled with gladness the hearts of even the gods. And that tiger among men, Nala, also had not his peer in the three worlds; for in beauty he was like Kandarpa himself in his embodied form. And moved by admiration, the heralds again and again celebrated the praises of Nala before Damayanti and those of Damayanti before the ruler of the Nishadhas. And repeatedly hearing of each other's virtues, they conceived an attachment towards each other not begot of sight. And that attachment, O son of Kunti, began to grow in strength. And then Nala was unable to control the love that was in his bosom. And he began to pass much of his time in solitude in the gardens adjoining the inner apartment of his palace. And there were a number of swans furnished with golden wings wandering in those woods. And from among them he caught one with his hands. And thereupon the sky-ranging one said unto

Nala, "Deserve I not to be slain by thee, O king. I will do something that is agreeable to thee. O king of the Nishadhas, I will speak of thee before Damayanti in such a way that she will not ever desire to have any other person." Thus addressed, the king liberated that swan, who rose on his golden wings.